Kids in the Kitchen

P.J. Tierney

GLOBAL COOKBOOK

Delicious Recipes from Seven Continents

KITCHEN INK

KITCHEN INK's passionate Kids in the Kitchen team of recipe creators, testers, editors, food stylists, photographers, and designers work tirelessly to create products that introduce kids to cooking. Having fun, making memories in the kitchen, and creating a delicious meal is what we are all about.

Our easy-to-follow, creative, and delicious recipes—kid-tested and parent-approved—include both healthy meals and special treats. Adult supervision and safety first are always important in the kitchen. We hope you enjoy our books as much as we have loved creating them.

Library of Congress Cataloging-in-Publication data is available.
ISBN 978-1-943016-22-8

First Edition
28 29 27 26 25   10 9 8 7 6 5 4 3 2 1

Printed in China

K TCHEN
INK

Kitchen Ink Publishing
114 John Street, #277
New York, NY 10038

Kitchen Ink books may be purchased for educational, business, or sales promotional use. For information, please email the Special Markets Department at sales@kitcheninkpublishing.com.

See what Kitchen Ink is up to, share recipes and tips, and shop our store—www.kitcheninkpublishing.com.

  kitcheninkpublishing

For Paul

My favorite travel buddy,
always.

**"I realized very early the power of food
to evoke memory, to bring people together,
to transport you to other places,
and I wanted to be a part of that."**

—José Andrés, Chef and Founder of World Central Kitchen

Introduction by P.J. Tierney

I love an adventure. Traveling around the world, meeting new people, tasting traditional cuisines, experiencing different cultures, and exploring art and celebrations makes me happy. How many countries have I visited? A lot! At age 12, my aunt and my grandmother "Momma" took me to Ireland and I knew then I wanted to travel around the globe. Momma was from County Mayo. At that time, I was not an adventurous eater, and Irish bread was my staple for 10 days. My family's delicious Irish Soda Bread recipe is on page 2. I prefer mine without caraway seeds.

From Europe, the delicious Pasta with Tomato Sauce Scarpariello (page 76) transports me back to the Piazza Navona, where I enjoyed eating delicious pasta while looking at the Neptune Fountain—one of Rome's more than 2,000 amazing fountains. A traditional UK recipe with a very odd name, Toad in the Hole (page 80), is sure to surprise everyone at the dinner table. Don't worry, no toads are on the ingredient list for this recipe.

Asia is so large and diverse. Securing a visa for Beijing was a challenge, but worth it to hike across the Great Wall of China. The Great Wall and Hong Kong's skyscrapers represent the old and new architecture. Wherever you are in China, food is tied to tradition. For good luck, make Birthday Noodles (page 74). Do not cut them because, according to tradition, long noodles represent a long life. Eat this dish on your birthday and you will have a long life.

The people of Indonesia are so welcoming. While visiting Bali, I experienced the simple pleasures of relaxation and love. In stark contrast to this is the bright lights, noise, and excitement of Bangkok. Both countries have amazing fresh food and I embraced vegetarianism (for a bit).

The cookbook's Thai Basil Tofu Stir Fry (page 58) is delicious and full of simple, fresh ingredients and spices.

Attending an amazing multiday wedding in India is an experience that's hard to top. I remember the celebration, the traditional clothing (I wore a custom silk sari), the henna tattoos, the friends, the food (so much food!), and the love. It was the first time I drank a lassi, and so I've included a refreshing Mango Lassi recipe (page 28).

I have traveled around Africa, including a whitewater rafting trip on the Nile River in Uganda, a Kenyan safari, and an exploration of Zanzibar, the spice island. The spice combination of cumin, turmeric, curry, and apricot with the beef and egg in Bobotie (page 61) is delicious. For Americans, it's a pumped-up version of a hamburger casserole.

A few more favorites: Caribbean islands, Cuba, Costa Rica, Grenada, Guatemala, Mexico, Panama, Bermuda, and of course Boston, MA in good old USA. A special sweet treat is the Boston Cream Pie (page 90) and no, it's not actually a pie. During colonial times, the words "cake" and "pie" were used interchangeably. Originally, the cake was baked in pie tins.

I look forward to eating ANZAC Biscuits (page 104) baked in a real Australian kitchen. These biscuits are named for the Australian and New Zealand Army Corps (ANZAC) created in World War I. The biscuits were sent to soldiers abroad because they kept well during naval transportation. There are no towns, cities, commercial industries, or permanent residents in Antarctica, the fifth largest continent. Sledging Biscuits (page 12), high in fat and energy, are a staple for scientists on expedition. These biscuits are dense and, in my opinion, need a topping to add flavor. I recommend Strawberry Jam (page 5).

I want everyone to experience the tastes of the world and I am making it easy for you to experience what the cool kids eat on different continents around the globe. No need to secure visas, no long flights, and no language barriers. Turn to the book's back inside cover and you will find your very own Culinary Passport. Add your photo to it and enter your information. Track the recipes you make, and take notes in your passport. Answer the journal questions and explore countries beyond these recipes.

If you are borrowing this book, NO FEAR! You will find a free passport to download on the Global Cookbook Series page at www.kitcheninkpublishing.com. The file will have the pages, not the stickers.

What Stickers?
As an incentive to create the recipes in this and future books in the Culinary Passport Series, you will find stickers in the passport. If the corresponding illustration is on a recipe page, complete the recipe, and add the sticker to your passport. It's just like when you travel to a different country and get a stamp in your passport. You can track your recipes and your journey.

The Chocolate Croissant recipe is from Austria—yes, Austria. Many think croissants are from France. Turn to page 8 for this recipe, and you will see a blue ribbon on the page. This recipe is a more challenging one and so once you complete it, you earn a sticker for your passport.

Preparing all recipes in a book is a challenge and will take time. You may want to pass on a recipe you think you won't like. You don't have to like every recipe, but make it and taste it. You might be surprised. Once you complete all recipes in the book, congratulations! You've earned the book's cover sticker to add to your Culinary Passport. Quite the accomplishment!

There are also stickers for traditional celebrations in China, France, Germany, India, Ireland, Italy, and Mexico. Prepare each recipe with a celebration graphic and add the sticker to your passport.

Global Cookbook, Delicious Recipes from Seven Continents, recipes are organized by breakfast, small plates, sides and snacks, entrees, and desserts. These are only suggestions. If you want to have a breakfast recipe for dinner, or eat dessert first, go right ahead! Maybe check with an adult on the desserts first.

We have just one world, and learning about cultures and traditions, and experiencing food from other countries is so important. It helps us all to understand that, as different as we are, there are so many similarities as well. Families around the world gather to share meals and to exchange stories. Some may have more than others, but the love is the same.

I am in awe of Chef José Andrés and his nonprofit World Central Kitchen (WCK). They serve chef-prepared meals to communities impacted by natural disasters and humanitarian crises. No matter where, WCK arrives with chefs, pots, and food to cook for those in need. At the end of this book, you will find additional information on how to support this amazing and wonderful organization.

Thanks for joining me on this culinary adventure.

Enjoy!

P.J. Tierney

A Note from the Kids in the Kitchen Team

Each recipe notes the number of servings 🍴 and the time needed to prepare the dish 🕐. Please note, the recommended chilling time for a dish may not be included in its active preparation time.

This cookbook includes easy recipes and those requiring a little more patience and skill. As you become more comfortable preparing recipes, it is important to be challenged and improve your kitchen skills.

An adult should be with you to assist, especially when using a knife and the stovetop, and when putting your delicious dishes into and bringing them out of the hot oven. It is up to the adult to decide when you can be more independent in the kitchen.

Step-by-step directions tell you what you need to prepare the dish. Read each recipe completely before you begin and make sure you have all the tools and ingredients you need. These recipes are written for kids all around the globe and both US measurements and metrics are included.

Sometimes a recipe may call for an ingredient you do not have. A substitution will be offered for an international ingredient that may be challenging to find. Please note if an ingredient is marked "optional," you can leave it out of the recipe if you choose.

If you are vegetarian, you will find recipes without meat or with suggestions to prepare meatless versions of the dish.

Everyone is excited to taste the food they have created BUT hit the brakes. Food is piping hot when removed from the oven. Always be patient and let the food cool before sampling. Your tongue will thank you.

Always clean up the kitchen when you are done and remember that more hands make light work. Have a cleanup party and everyone is rewarded with dessert.

Contents

Breakfast

Small Plates, Sides & Snacks

Entrées

Desserts

Recipes by Continent

Asia

Africa

North America

South America

Europe

Australia and Oceania

Antarctica

Breakfast

Irish Soda Bread

 55 minutes   1 loaf

Ireland

Ingredients

4 cups (960 milliliters) all-purpose flour

1 teaspoon (5 milliliters) baking soda

1 teaspoon (5 milliliters) salt

1 tablespoon (15 milliliters) granulated sugar

2 cups (480 milliliters) buttermilk

1 cup (240 milliliters) raisins or currants, optional

½ teaspoon (2.5 milliliters) to 2 teaspoons (10 milliliters)

Caraway seeds to taste, optional

Directions

1. Preheat the oven to 450°F (230°C). Line a large baking sheet with parchment paper and set aside.

2. In a large mixing bowl, sift together the flour, soda, salt, and sugar. Whisk together until well combined.

3. Make a well in the center of the dry ingredients; pour in the buttermilk. Mix together using a rubber spatula for about 30 seconds, until the mixture forms a loose dough. Don't overwork the dough – overmixing can make the interior rubbery. Add the raisins and caraway seeds (if using) and mix in quickly, about 10 seconds more.

4. Turn the dough out onto a lightly floured work surface. Knead briefly until the dough sticks together, about 3 to 4 turns. Form the dough into a ball. Transfer the dough to the prepared baking sheet.

5. Carefully score a cross in the top of the loaf using a large serrated knife, or a sharp chef's knife, to about 1-inch (2.5 centimeters) depth. Immediately transfer it to the preheated oven.

6. Bake for 40 to 45 minutes, or until the bread is split at the cross, and the crust is well browned. The loaf should be well risen and have a hollow sound when tapped on the bottom with your knuckles.

7. Let bread cool slightly before slicing; serve warm. Top with butter and/or jam.

TIP

Top with a flavored butter see page 14-18 and strawberry jam on page 5.

Strawberry Jam

 40 minutes   24 servings

USA

Ingredients

1 pound (454 grams) fresh strawberries, washed, hulls removed, and sliced

1 ½ cups (360 milliliters) granulated white sugar

2 tablespoons (30 milliliters) lemon juice

½ teaspoon (2.5 milliliters) lemon zest, optional

Directions

1. In a medium saucepan over medium heat, add the strawberries and sugar and mix well. Stir continually to bring to a boil.

2. Once boiling, add the lemon juice and zest, if using.

3. Boil for about 15 minutes, or until the jam reaches 220°F (104°C).

4. Stir often, to make sure the jam doesn't burn.

5. Pour into a jar and allow to cool.

6. Cover and refrigerate.

Polynesian Fruit Salad

 20 minutes

 6 to 8 servings

French Polynesia

Ingredients

1 cup (240 milliliters) strawberries, stemmed and sliced in half

20 ounces (566.99 grams) of pineapple, cut into chunks

1 papaya, peeled, seeded, and cut into chunks

4 kiwi's, peeled and cut into chunks

1 tablespoon (15 milliliters) lemon juice

¼ teaspoon (1.2 milliliters) poppy seeds, optional

1 tablespoon (15 milliliters) coconut, shredded, optional

Directions

1. In a large bowl, add strawberries, pineapple, papaya, and kiwi and gently combine.
2. Add lemon juice and gently stir.
3. If using, sprinkle poppy seeds and coconut over salad and toss gently.

Chocolate Croissants

 6 hours 10 minutes   8 servings

Austria

Ingredients

4 cups (960 milliliters) flour

½ cup (120 milliliters) water

½ cup (120 milliliters) milk

¼ cup (60 milliliters) sugar

2 teaspoons (10 milliliters) salt

1 packet instant dry yeast

3 tablespoons (45 milliliters) unsalted butter, softened

1 ¼ cups (300 milliliters) cold unsalted butter, cut into ½-inch (1.25-centimeter) thick slices

1 egg, beaten

2 bars sweetened chocolate

Directions

1. In a large bowl, mix the flour, water, milk, sugar, salt, yeast, and butter.
2. Once the dough starts to clump, turn it out onto a clean counter.
3. Lightly knead the dough and form it into a ball, making sure not to over-knead it.
4. Cover the dough with plastic wrap and refrigerate for 1 hour.
5. Slice the cold butter into thirds vertically.
6. Place another piece of parchment on top of the butter, and beat it with a rolling pin.
7. Keeping the parchment paper on the butter, use a rolling pin to roll the butter into a 7-inch (18-centimeter) square, ½-inch (1.25-centimeter) thick. If necessary, use a knife to trim the edges and place the trimmings back on top of the butter and continue to roll into a square.
8. Transfer the butter layer to the fridge.
9. To roll out the dough, lightly flour the counter. Place the dough on the counter and push the rolling pin once vertically into the dough and once horizontally to form four pieces.
10. Roll out each corner and form a 10-inch (25-centimeter) square.
11. Place the butter layer on top of the dough and fold the sides of the dough over the butter, enclosing it completely. Roll the dough with a rolling pin to seal the seams, making sure to lengthen the dough, rather than widening it.
12. Transfer the dough to a baking sheet and cover with plastic wrap. Refrigerate for 1 hour.
13. Roll out the dough on a floured surface until it's 8 x 24 inches (20 x 61 centimeters).
14. Fold the top half down to the middle, and brush off any excess flour.
15. Fold the bottom half over the top and turn the dough clockwise to the left. This completes the first turn.
16. Cover and refrigerate for 1 hour. Roll out the dough again two more times, completing three turns in total and refrigerating for 1 hour in between each turn. If at any time the dough or butter begins to soften, stop and transfer back to the fridge.

17. After the final turn, cover the dough with plastic wrap and refrigerate overnight.

18. To form the croissants, cut the dough in half. Place one half in the fridge.

19. Flour the surface and roll out the dough into a long narrow strip, about 8 x 40 inches (20 x 101 centimeters). With a knife, trim the edges of the dough.

20. Cut the dough into 4 rectangles.

21. Place the chocolate on the edge of the dough and roll tightly to enclose it in the dough.

22. Place the croissants on a baking sheet, seam side down.

23. Repeat with the other half of the dough.

24. Brush the croissants with the beaten egg. Save the rest of the egg wash in the fridge for later.

25. Place the croissants in a warm place to rise for 1 to 2 hours.

26. Preheat oven to 400°F (200°C).

27. Once the croissants have proofed, brush them with one more layer of egg wash.

28. Bake for 15 minutes or until golden brown and cooked through. Serve warm.

TIP
To proof - allowing dough to rise after is has been shaped and before it is baked.

Sledging Biscuits

 50 minutes   8 servings

Antarctica

Ingredients

1 ¼ cups (300 milliliters) whole wheat flour

½ teaspoon (2.5 milliliters) baking soda

½ teaspoon (2.5 milliliters) salt

2 tablespoons (30 milliliters) butter, unsalted

3 tablespoons (45 milliliters) and 1 teaspoon (5 milliliters) cold water

TIP
Top with a flavored butter
see page 14-18 and strawberry
jam on page 5.

Directions

1. Preheat oven to 375°F (190°C).
2. In a medium bowl, rub the butter and flour together forming a fine consistent crumb. Add the baking soda and salt, and mix well.
3. Add a little of the water and knead the mixture to a soft flexible dough, adding a little water at a time to get the right consistency. Take your time kneading to combine well. Roll dough into a ball.
4. Place the ball of dough on a lightly floured surface and roll it out to just under half an inch thick and cut into rectangles. Yields 8 approximately 2-inch x 3-inch (5-centimeters x 7.6 centimeters) biscuits.
5. Prick the surface of the biscuits lightly with a fork and place on a baking sheet lined with parchment.
6. Place in the preheated oven and bake for 20 minutes. The biscuits should be golden in color and, if needed, placed back in the oven for an additional 5 minutes to achieve this color.
7. Remove from the oven and let cool.

Flavored Butters

 15 minutes   10 servings

Orange Butter

USA

Ingredients

½ cup (120 milliliters) butter

1 tablespoon (15 milliliters) powdered sugar

½ teaspoon (2.5 milliliters) orange peel, finely shredded

1 teaspoon (5 milliliters) orange juice

TIP
Serve in half
an orange.

Directions

1. In a medium bowl, combine the butter, powdered sugar, orange peel, and orange juice and mix well.
2. If using half an orange as a serving bowl, fill it now.
3. Serve at room temperature.

How to hollow out an orange to make a fruit bowl
1. Cut both ends of a large orange.
2. Using a spoon, separate the flesh of the orange from the rind.
3. Push all the flesh out of the orange.
4. Remove the orange flesh from one of the ends you cut off.
5. Fill the bowl with orange butter.

Apple Spice Butter

Ingredients

5 ⅓ tablespoons (78 milliliters) butter, salted or unsalted, room temperature

2 tablespoons (30 milliliters) honey

1 teaspoon (5 milliliters) Apple Pie Spice

⅓ cup (80 milliliters) powdered sugar

USA

Pizza Butter

Ingredients

5 ⅓ tablespoons (78 milliliters) butter, salted or unsalted, room temperature

1 tablespoon (15 milliliters) basil leaves, shredded

1 tablespoon (15 milliliters) sundried tomato, finely chopped

½ garlic clove, grated

¼ teaspoon (1.2 milliliters) sea salt

Garlic & Parsley Butter

USA

Ingredients

5 ⅓ tablespoons (78 milliliters) butter, salted or unsalted, room temperature

2 tablespoons (30 milliliters) fresh parsley, finely chopped

1 garlic clove, crushed

Directions

1. Take 5 ⅓ tablespoons (78 milliliters) of butter from the fridge for an hour to soften. Beat the butter with a wooden spoon until it is soft and creamy, then beat in any of the herbs.

2. Tip the flavored butter onto a square of baking parchment or cling film, roll it around the butter to form a sausage shape, then twist the ends to seal. The butter is now ready to be stored for up to 3 days in the fridge or up to a month in the freezer.

Pain Perdu

 25 minutes   4 servings

France

Ingredients

4 slices egg bread

1 egg

5 tablespoons (75 milliliters) unsalted butter

3 tablespoons (45 milliliters) white sugar

1 pinch salt

½ teaspoon (2.5 milliliters) ground cinnamon

1 pinch ground nutmeg

⅓ cup (80 milliliters) all-purpose flour

¾ cup (175 milliliters) milk

¾ teaspoon (3.75 milliliters) vanilla extract

TIP
Brioche, French bread, or Italian bread are all great substitutes for egg bread.

Directions

1. Place bread slices on a wire rack to dry while preparing batter.

2. Melt 3 tablespoons (45 milliliters) butter in a saucepan over medium-low heat and allow to cool slightly.

3. Whisk egg in a shallow bowl. Whisk sugar, salt, cinnamon, and nutmeg into egg. When butter has cooled slightly, slowly drizzle it into egg mixture while whisking. Add flour to egg mixture, a little at a time, until a smooth and thick paste forms. Slowly blend in milk and vanilla; whisk until just smooth and set aside.

4. Heat remaining butter in a large skillet over medium heat.

5. Dip a bread slice in batter and allow to soak for no more than 30 seconds. Remove from batter and allow excess to drip back into the bowl. Place battered slice in the hot skillet. Repeat with remaining bread slices.

6. Cook bread slices until golden, 2 to 3 minutes per side. Serve immediately.

Belgian Waffles

 30 minutes   10 waffles

Belgium

Ingredients

2 cups (480 milliliters) all-purpose flour

¾ cup (175 milliliters) sugar

3 ½ teaspoons (17.5 milliliters) baking powder

2 large eggs, separated

1 cup (240 milliliters) butter, melted

1 teaspoon (5 milliliters) vanilla extract

Toppings - fresh fruit and powdered sugar, Nutella, whipped cream, or syrup

Directions

1. Preheat a waffle maker.
2. In a large bowl, combine flour, sugar, and baking powder.
3. In a medium bowl, lightly beat egg yolks. Add milk, butter, and vanilla and mix well.
4. Stir the wet ingredients into the dry and combine.
5. In a small bowl, beat egg whites until stiff peaks form; fold into batter.
6. Pour the batter into the preheated waffle maker and cook until golden brown. Serve warm with the topping of your choice.

Huevos Rancheros with Refried Beans

 40 minutes   4 servings

Mexico

Ingredients

Pico de Gallo

2 medium ripe tomatoes, chopped (approximately 1 ½ cups (360 milliliters)

¼ cup (60 milliliters) white onion, finely chopped

¼ cup (60 milliliters) fresh cilantro, chopped

2 tablespoons (30 milliliters) lime juice

¼ teaspoon (1.2 milliliters) fine-grain sea salt

Tortillas and Eggs

1 ½ cups (360 milliliters) of red salsa, choose your favorite

4 teaspoons (20 milliliters) extra-virgin olive oil, divided

4 eggs

4 corn tortillas

½ cup (120 milliliters) Monterey Jack cheese, shredded

Freshly ground black pepper

Optional garnishes: additional cheese of your choice, sliced avocado, and hot sauce

Refried Beans

2 teaspoons (10 milliliters) extra-virgin olive oil

¼ cup (60 milliliters) white onion, finely chopped

¼ teaspoon (1.2 milliliters) fine-grain sea salt

1 teaspoon (5 milliliters) ground cumin

15 ounces (425 grams) black or pinto beans, rinsed and drained

¼ cup (60 milliliters) water

Freshly ground black pepper, to taste

½ teaspoon (2.5 milliliters) lime juice

Directions

1. To prepare the pico de gallo: In a medium bowl, combine the tomatoes, onion, cilantro, lime juice, and salt. Stir to combine, then set the bowl aside for later.

2. To cook the beans: In a small saucepan over medium heat, warm the olive oil until shimmering. Add the onions and salt. Cook, stirring occasionally, until the onions have softened and are turning translucent, about 3 to 6 minutes.

3. Add the cumin and cook, stirring constantly, until fragrant, about 30 seconds. Pour in the drained beans and water. Stir, cover, and cook for 5 minutes. Reduce the heat to low, then remove the lid and use a potato masher or the back of a fork to mash up at least half of the beans. Continue to cook the beans, uncovered, stirring often, for 2 to 3 more minutes, until thickened.

4. Remove the pot from the heat and stir in the pepper and lime juice. Taste and add more salt, pepper or lime juice if necessary. If the beans seem dry, add a very small splash of water and stir to combine. Cover until ready to serve.

5. Meanwhile, warm the salsa. Pour the salsa into a medium saucepan over medium heat. Bring the salsa to a simmer, stirring occasionally, and then reduce the heat to low until ready to serve.

6. In a small skillet over medium heat, warm each tortilla individually, flipping as necessary. Spread the black bean mixture over each tortilla and place each tortilla on an individual plate. If using Jack cheese, sprinkle it over the tortillas. Set aside.

7. To fry the eggs: In the same skillet over medium heat, pour in 1 teaspoon (5 milliliters) olive oil and wait until it's shimmering. Carefully crack an egg and pour it into the skillet without breaking the yolk. Fry the egg, lifting and tilting the pan occasionally to redistribute the oil, until the whites are set and the yolk is cooked to your preferred level of doneness. Place the fried egg on top of a prepared tortilla and repeat with the remaining eggs.

8. Spoon about one-fourth of the warmed salsa across each dish, avoiding the egg yolk. Use a slotted spoon or fork to do the same with the pico de gallo, leaving the messy tomato juices behind. Sprinkle with freshly ground black pepper and add any additional garnishes you might like.

Orange Maple Syrup

 40 minutes

 2 cups (480 milliliters)

USA

Ingredients

1 teaspoon (5 milliliters) orange zest, finely grated

½ cup (120 milliliters) amber maple syrup

¼ teaspoon(1.2 milliliters) kosher salt

6 tablespoons (90 milliliters) cold unsalted butter, cut into pieces

Directions

1. In a small saucepan over medium-high heat bring the orange juice to a boil; reduce the heat to maintain a steady simmer and cook until slightly syrupy and liquid reduces by half, 8 to 10 minutes.

2. Add the maple syrup, orange zest, and salt and cook 1 more minute.

3. Remove from the heat, and whisk in the butter one piece at a time.

Mango Lassi

 5 minutes

 2 servings

India

Ingredients

1 ½ cup (360 milliliters) mangos, rinsed, chilled, peeled, and cubed

¾ cup (175 milliliters) plain yogurt

¾ cup (175 milliliters) milk, or replace with water

1 ½ to 3 tablespoons (22.5 to 45 milliliters) sugar, to taste

¼ teaspoon (1.2 milliliters) cardamom powder

1 teaspoon (5 milliliters) chopped nuts, optional topping

Whipped cream, optional topping

Directions

1. Add to a blender the mango, yogurt, milk or water (if using), cardamom powder, and sugar.
2. Blend until the Mango Lassi is super smooth. It should be thick and easy to pour.
3. Pour into two glasses and if you prefer it colder refrigerate for an hour.

Small Plates, Sides & Snacks

Fried Green Plantains

 40 minutes   4 servings

Haiti

Ingredients

1 green plantain, peeled and cut into 1-inch (2.5-centimeter) thick slices

⅔ cup (160 milliliters) canola oil

1 cup (240 milliliters) water

½ teaspoon (5 milliliters) salt

Directions

1. In a nonstick medium pan, over medium heat, add the oil and the plantain slices. Slices should not touch.

2. Fry plantains 3 minutes and then turn over and fry for another 3 minutes.

3. Remove each plantain from the pan and place it on a paper towel.

4. Prior to cooling, transfer a plantain to a small plate and place another small plate on top of it. Press down to mash the plantain. Repeat with each plantain slice.

5. In a small bowl, add the water and salt and dip each plantain into the salt water.

6. Reheat the pan over medium-low heat, add the plantains and flip as they cook, 5 minutes per side. Each should be golden in color and hard on each side.

7. Repeat until all plantains are cooked. Remove from pan and place on a paper towel to drain excess oil.

Maple-Chia Chewy Bars

 45 minutes

 12 servings

Canada

Ingredients

Coconut butter or oil, for the pan

½ cup (120 milliliters) chia seeds

1 ½ cup (360 milliliters) quick-cooking oats

¾ cup (175 milliliters) maple sugar

½ cup (120 milliliters) dried fruits and/or berries, your choice (cranberries, raisins, etc.)

½ cup (120 milliliters) unsalted roasted almonds, crushed

3 tablespoons (45 milliliters) flour

¼ teaspoon (1.2 milliliters) baking powder

¼ teaspoon (1.2 milliliters) salt

¼ teaspoon (1.2 milliliters) ground cinnamon

¼ cup (60 milliliters) virgin coconut oil, at room temperature

½ cup (120 milliliters) almond milk or orange juice

Directions

1. Preheat oven to 350°F (180°C).

2. Line a 28 x 20 cm (11 x 8 inch) rectangular pan with parchment paper, enough to hang over the edges to simplify removal. Oil and set aside.

3. In a large bowl, combine all dry ingredients (chia, oats, maple sugar, dried fruits and/or berries, almonds, flour, baking powder, salt, and cinnamon). Use a wooden spoon to incorporate the coconut oil and almond milk or orange juice.

4. Spread the mixture in the pan and press down very firmly. Bake for 35 to 40 minutes or until golden brown. Let stand 15 minutes, then cut into bars in the pan. Remove and allow to cool completely.

Balsamic Bruschetta

 20 minutes   8 servings

Italy

Ingredients

1 loaf French bread, cut into ¼-inch (0.6-centimeter) slices 1 tablespoon (15 milliliters) extra-virgin olive oil

8 roma (plum) tomatoes, diced

⅓ cup (80 milliliters) chopped fresh basil

1 ounce (28 grams) Parmesan cheese, freshly grated

2 cloves garlic, minced

1 tablespoon (15 milliliters) good quality balsamic vinegar

2 teaspoons (10 milliliters) extra-virgin olive oil

¼ teaspoon (1.2 milliliters) kosher salt

¼ teaspoon (1.2 milliliters) freshly ground black pepper

Directions

1. Gather all ingredients.
2. Preheat oven to 400°F (200°C).
3. Brush bread slices on both sides lightly with 1 tablespoon (15 milliliters) oil and place on large baking sheet. Toast bread until golden, 5 to 10 minutes, turning halfway through.
4. Meanwhile, toss together tomatoes, basil, Parmesan cheese, and garlic in a bowl.
5. Mix in balsamic vinegar, 2 teaspoons (10 milliliters) olive oil, kosher salt, and pepper.
6. Spoon tomato mixture onto toasted bread slices.
7. Serve immediately.

Khorovats
(Armenian Grilled Vegetable Salad)

 30 minutes   4 servings

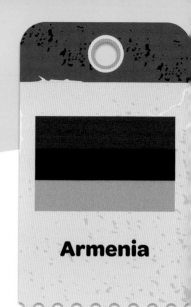

Armenia

Ingredients

2 medium eggplants

3 red bell peppers

2 medium tomatoes, chopped into ½-inch (1.25-centimeter) pieces

½ large onion, peeled, cut into thirds lengthwise and thinly sliced crosswise

¾ cups (175 milliliters) flat-leaf parsley, chopped

⅓ cup (80 milliliters) lemon juice

2 tablespoons (30 milliliters) extra-virgin olive oil

1 ½ tablespoons (22.5 milliliters) kosher salt

1 tablespoon (15 milliliters) paprika

¼ teaspoon (1.2 milliliters) black pepper

Garlic, cilantro, basil – optional additional herbs for flavor, to taste

TIP
Have an adult start the grill and place and turn the vegetables on the grill.

Directions

1. Preheat the grill to medium heat, about 350°F (180°C).

2. With a fork, poke holes in the skin of the eggplants in three or four places. Place the tomatoes, eggplants, and bell peppers on the grill. Close the lid.

3. Check on the vegetables every once in a while and turn them as needed.

4. Cook the vegetables for about 20 minutes or until they are soft and start to collapse. The vegetables should be cooked through and tender.

5. Arrange on a platter and garnish with fresh herbs and chopped red onion.

To Make the Salad

1. Transfer the cooked vegetables from the grill into a bowl.
   Cover with a lid and let it stand until the vegetables are cool enough to handle (5 to 10 minutes).

2. Remove the skin from the vegetables and chop into chunks.
   Drain the liquid as needed.

3. Transfer into a salad bowl and add the garlic, cilantro, parsley, basil, and olive oil, if using. Season with salt. Serve warm.

Irio (Mashed Potatoes, Corn, and Peas)

 30 minutes   5 servings

Kenya

Ingredients

2 ½ pounds (1.13 kilograms) potatoes

1 ½ cups (360 milliliters) green peas

1 ½ cups (360 milliliters) corn

2 tablespoons (30 milliliters) butter

Salt and pepper, to taste

TIP
Serve with Peri Peri Chicken.
See page 64.

Directions

1. Peel the potatoes and cut each into evenly sized chunks, about 1-inch (2.5-centimeters) thick.

2. In a large pot, place the potatoes, peas, and corn and add enough water to cover the potatoes.

3. Cook on medium-high for about 15 to 20 minutes or until the potatoes are tender when stuck with a fork.

4. Drain the excess water (if any) but leave about 4 tablespoons (60 milliliters) inside the pot for easy mashing.

5. Season with salt and black pepper, and mash with a wooden spoon or potato masher.

6. Stir the butter into the mixture.

7. Serve hot.

Egg Rolls

 35 minutes   12 servings

China

Ingredients

1 pound (454 grams) ground pork

1 teaspoon (5 milliliters) ground ginger

1 teaspoon (5 milliliters) garlic powder

1 quart (0.9 liters vegetable oil, for frying

1 tablespoon (15 milliliters) all-purpose flour

1 tablespoon (15 milliliters) water

3 cups (720 milliliters) coleslaw mix

12 egg roll wrappers

Directions

1. In a medium skillet over medium heat, cook the pork, breaking it up as it cooks. When it is halfway cooked, sprinkle the ground ginger and garlic powder over the pork and stir to coat the meat evenly. Continue to cook until the pork is no longer pink. Set aside.

2. In another large heavy pot, heat oil to 375°F (190°C) or medium high heat. While the oil is heating, combine the flour and water in a bowl until they form a paste. In a separate bowl, combine the coleslaw mix and reserved pork mixture. Mix it all together.

3. Lay out one egg roll skin with a corner pointed toward you. Place about ¼ to ⅓ cup (60 to 80 milliliters) of the pork mixture on the egg roll paper and fold the corner up over the mixture. Fold left and right corners toward the center and continue to roll. Brush a bit of the flour paste on the final corner to help seal the egg roll.

4. Place the egg rolls into the heated oil and fry, turning occasionally, until golden brown. Remove from the oil and drain on paper towels or a rack.

Carrot Quiche

 1 hour

 6 servings

France

Ingredients

1 ½ cups (360 milliliters) all-purpose flour

½ teaspoon (2.5 milliliters) salt

½ cup (120 milliliters) (one stick) unsalted butter, chilled and cut into 8 pieces

1 cup (240 milliliters) and 3 tablespoons (45 milliliters) half-and-half, divided

10 ounces (283.5 grams) carrots, shredded

½ cup (120 milliliters) orange juice

3 eggs

½ teaspoon (2.5 milliliters) salt

¼ teaspoon (1.2 milliliters) pepper

½ teaspoon (2.5 milliliters) ground nutmeg

4 ounces (110 grams) cheddar cheese, grated

1. Preheat the oven to 400°F (200°C).

For the Crust:

2. In a food processor, add the flour and salt and pulse several times. Add the butter and pulse several more times and then process for about 1 minute. Add 3 tablespoons (45 milliliters) of half-and-half and pulse several more times until the mixture is smooth.

3. Place the mixture into a pie pan. Press the crust firmly into the pan with your fingers, pressing up the sides of the pan. Bake the crust for approximately 12 minutes.

4. As the crust is prebaking, in a saucepan on medium heat, place the shredded carrots and orange juice and cover. Heat on medium for 10 minutes.

5. Once the crust is prebaked, in a small bowl, whisk together the eggs, remaining cup of half-and-half, salt, pepper, and nutmeg.

6. Add the cooked carrots and egg mixture into the crust and sprinkle with the cheese.

7. Bake for 20 minutes. Allow to cool slightly before slicing and serving.

Pierogis

 2 hours

 12 servings (5 pierogis per person)

Poland

Ingredients

Potato Filling

2 pounds (908 grams) russet potatoes, 5 medium potatoes, peeled

½ teaspoon (2.5 milliliters) salt

2 tablespoons (30 milliliters) unsalted butter, melted

2 ounces (57 grams) cream cheese, softened

¾ cup (180 milliliters) mozzarella cheese, shredded

¾ cup mozzarella cheese, shredded

Scallions, chopped, for garnish, optional

Dough

1 cup (240 milliliters) warm water

¼ cup (60 milliliters) whole milk

2 tablespoons (30 milliliters) sour cream

3 tablespoons (45 milliliters) extra light virgin olive oil, or vegetable oil

1 large egg

1 ½ teaspoons (7.5 milliliters) fine sea salt, plus more for cooking

4 cups (960 milliliters) all-purpose flour

Toppings

4 ounces (113 grams) bacon, chopped

2 tablespoons (30 milliliters) unsalted butter

Sour cream, optional for serving

Directions

1. In a large pot, over medium-high heat, add potatoes and enough water to cover and bring to a boil. Continue to cook 25 minutes or until easily pierced with a fork. Drain and cool five minutes then mash potatoes until smooth.

2. Add in ½ teaspoon (2.5 milliliters) salt, 2 tablespoons (30 milliliters) melted butter, and 2 ounces (57 grams) cream cheese. Mash in ¾ cup (180 milliliters) shredded mozzarella cheese. Partially cover and set aside while rolling out the dough.

3. In a large mixing bowl, whisk together 1 cup (240 milliliters) warm water, ¼ cup (60 milliliters) milk, 2 tablespoons (30 milliliters) sour cream, 1 egg, 3 tablespoons (45 milliliters) oil, and 1 ½ teaspoon (7.5 milliliters) salt until blended.

4. Add 2 cups (480 milliliters) of flour and mix until combined, add the remaining flour ½ a cup (120 milliliters) at a time, mixing and scraping down the sides of the bowl. When the dough no longer sticks to the sides of the bowl or your hands it is ready to be kneaded.

5. Remove the dough from the bowl and place on a lightly floured surface. Knead for 2-3 minutes or until the dough is smooth and elastic. Cover dough with a damp cloth and let rest for 30 minutes.

6. Divide the dough into 2 pieces. On a floured surface roll out to 1/8-inch (0.3-centimeter) thickness.

7. Use a 3-inch (7.6-centimeter) diameter round cookie cutter to cut circles from the dough. Keep cuts as close as possible to conserve dough. Add ½ tablespoon (7.5 milliliters) of potatoes centered on each round.

8. Pull the two edges of the dough together and pinch tightly to seal.

9. In a medium skillet, sauté bacon. Once crisp melt 2 tablespoons (30 milliliters) butter and remove from heat. This is the bacon topping to be drizzled over the cooked pierogis.

10. Bring a large pot of salted water to a boil. Add the pierogis in batches. Cook for approximately 2 minutes or until the pierogi's float to the top. Using a slotted spoon or strainer remove from the pot and place in a bowl and drizzle with the bacon topping and sprinkle with scallions.

Greek Salad

 15 minutes   4 servings

Greece

Ingredients

Dressing

¼ cup (60 milliliters) extra-virgin olive oil

3 tablespoons (45 milliliters) red wine vinegar

1 garlic clove, minced

½ teaspoon (2.5 milliliters) dried oregano, more for sprinkling

¼ teaspoon (1.2 milliliters) Dijon mustard

¼ teaspoon (1.2 milliliters) sea salt

Freshly ground black pepper

For the Salad

1 cucumber, cut lengthwise, seeded, and sliced ¼-inch (0.6-centimeters) thick

1 green bell pepper, chopped into 1-inch (2.5-centimeter) pieces

2 cups (480 milliliters) cherry tomatoes, halved

5 ounces (142 grams) feta cheese, cut into ½-inch (1.25-centimeter) cubes

⅓ cup (80 milliliters) thinly sliced red onion

⅓ cup (80 milliliters) pitted Kalamata olives

⅓ cup (80 milliliters) fresh mint leaves

Directions

1. In a small bowl, whisk together the olive oil, vinegar, garlic, oregano, mustard, salt, and several grinds of pepper.

2. On a large platter, arrange the cucumber, green pepper, cherry tomatoes, feta cheese, red onions, and olives. Drizzle with the dressing and very gently toss. Sprinkle with a few generous pinches of oregano and top with the mint leaves. Season to taste and serve.

Empanadas

 30 minutes

 4 servings

Spain

Ingredients

For the Dough

3 cups (720 milliliters) all-purpose flour, plus more for surface

1 teaspoon (5 milliliters) kosher salt

1 teaspoon (5 milliliters) baking powder

½ cup (120 milliliters) cold butter, cut into cubes

¾ cup (175 milliliters) water

1 large egg

1 tablespoon (15 milliliters) extra-virgin olive oil

1 yellow onion, chopped

2 cloves garlic, minced

1 pound (454 grams) ground beef, chicken, or 2 cups (480 milliliters) cheese

1 tablespoon (15 milliliters) tomato paste

1 teaspoon (5 milliliters) oregano

1 teaspoon (5 milliliters) cumin

½ teaspoon (2.5 milliliters) paprika

Kosher salt

Freshly ground black pepper

½ cup (120 milliliters) tomatoes, chopped

½ cup (120 milliliters) pickled jalapeños, chopped

1 ¼ cups (300 milliliters) cheddar cheese, shredded

1 ¼ cups (300 milliliters) Monterey Jack cheese, shredded

Egg wash, for brushing

Fresh cilantro, chopped for garnish

Sour cream, for serving

Directions

1. In a large bowl, whisk together flour, salt, and baking powder. Cut butter into flour using your hands or a pastry cutter until pea sized.

2. In a small bowl, add water and egg and mix into large bowl until a dough forms.

3. Lightly flour counter and knead dough until smooth, about 5 minutes. Wrap in plastic wrap and refrigerate for at least 1 hour.

4. Preheat oven to 400°F (200°C) and line two large baking sheets with parchment paper.

5. In a large skillet over medium heat, heat oil. Add onion and cook until soft, about 5 minutes, then add garlic and cook until fragrant, 1 minute more. Add ground beef and cook, breaking meat up with a wooden spoon, until no longer pink, 5 minutes. Drain fat.

6. Return pan to medium heat, and stir tomato paste into beef. Add oregano, cumin, and paprika, and season with salt and pepper. Add tomatoes and jalapeños and cook until warmed through, about 3 minutes. Remove from heat and let cool slightly.

7. Place dough on a lightly floured surface and divide in half. Roll one half out to ¼-inch (0.6-centimeters) thick. Using a 4.5-inch (11.25-centimeters) round cookie cutter, cut out rounds. Repeat with remaining dough. Reroll scraps once to cut out more rounds.

8. Lightly moisten outer edge of a dough round with water and place about 2 tablespoons (30 milliliters) filling in center and top with cheddar and Monterey cheeses. Fold dough in half over filling. Use a fork to crimp edges together. Repeat with remaining filling and dough.

9. Place empanadas on prepared baking sheets and brush with egg wash. Bake until golden and filling is warmed through, about 25 minutes. Garnish with cilantro and serve with sour cream.

TIP
For the filling, you decide: beef, chicken, or cheese.

Entrées

Pad Krapow (Thai Basil Tofu Stir Fry)

 15 minutes   2 servings

Thailand

Ingredients

16 ounces (454 grams) extra firm tofu

2 tablespoons (30 milliliters) avocado oil

½ large red bell pepper, sliced

¾ cup (180 milliliters) green beans, cut into ½-inch (1.25-centimeter) pieces

½ medium onion, chopped

1 cup (240 milliliters) Thai holy basil or star anise

Salt and pepper to taste

Sauce

3 tablespoons (45 milliliters) dark soy sauce

2 ½ teaspoons (12.5 milliliters) brown sugar

4 garlic cloves, chopped

¼ teaspoon (1.2 milliliters) ginger, grated

½ teaspoon (2.5 milliliters) Thai chili pepper flakes, optional for spice

TIP
Top it off
with a fried egg.

Directions

1. Wrap the tofu in a paper towel and with your clean hands squeeze out as much water as you can. Once drained, remove the paper towel and crumble the tofu with your hands.

2. In a medium skillet over medium-high heat add the oil and once hot, add the tofu crumbles and sauté until it becomes dry, approximately 5 minutes.

3. Add the sauce, pepper, beans, and onions and saute for five minutes or until the vegetables are cooked but still crispy.

4. Season with salt and pepper to taste.

5. Turn off the heat and stir in the Thai basil and mix it until the basil wilts.

6. Serve over rice.

TIP
If you want some crunch in this recipe, add peanuts or cashews to it.

Bobotie

 55 minutes   8 servings

South Africa

Ingredients

1 cup (240 milliliters) milk

2 slices white bread, crusts removed and broken into pieces

2 tablespoons (30 milliliters) oil

1 onion, chopped

2 garlic cloves, crushed

1 large carrot, grated

1 teaspoon (5 milliliters) turmeric

1 teaspoon (5 milliliters) curry powder

1 teaspoon (5 milliliters) cumin

1 pound (0.45 kilograms) ground beef

2 tablespoons (30 milliliters) chutney/apricot jam

½ cup (120 milliliters) water or beef broth

4 bay leaves

Salt to taste

Pepper to taste

For the Topping

½ cup (120 milliliters) milk

2 eggs

Salt to taste

Pepper taste

Directions

1. Preheat oven to 350°F (180°C).

2. In a medium bowl, soak the bread in milk and set aside.

3. In a large skillet, heat oil, add chopped onion, and sauté for 4 to 5 minutes. Add garlic and sauté for 1 minute. Add grated carrot and cook for 3 to 4 minutes. Add turmeric, curry powder, and cumin, and cook for 1 minute.

4. Add the beef. Cook the ground beef until it is no longer pink, stirring occasionally. Add the chutney and stir. Add ½ cup (120 milliliters) of water (or beef broth) and simmer for 5 to 10 minutes.

5. Squeeze the milk from the bread, reserving the milk for later. Add the bread to the meat mixture and mix well.

6. Spread the mixture evenly into an ovenproof dish.

7. To the remaining milk add another ½ cup (120 milliliters) of milk, and add 2 eggs, salt, and pepper. Whisk until combined. Pour over the meat mixture and arrange bay leaves on top.

8. Bake for 30 to 35 minutes or until golden and egg layer is set.

Peri Peri Chicken

 1 hour 15 minutes   2 servings

Mozambique

Ingredients

Chicken

4 chicken leg quarters (use drumsticks, bone-in thighs, or whole chicken)

1 teaspoon (5 milliliters) salt

1 teaspoon (5 milliliters) pepper

1 teaspoon (5 milliliters) smoked paprika

Oil for basting

Peri Peri Sauce

3 shallots, chopped

6 garlic cloves, chopped

1 red bell pepper, chopped

10 Thai chilis, optional, this adds the spice

2 bay leaves

⅓ cup (80 milliliters) olive oil

4 tablespoons (60 milliliters) tomato paste

1.5 tablespoons (22.5 milliliters) rice vinegar

1 lemon, rind and juice

1 tablespoon (15 milliliters) dried oregano

1.5 teaspoon (7.5 milliliters) salt

2 teaspoons (10 milliliters) smoked paprika

TIP

Prepare the sauce and marinate the chicken a day prior to cooking.

Directions

1. In a blender or food processor, add shallots, garlic, bell pepper, chilis, bay leaves, tomato paste, vinegar, oregano, lemon, oregano, and paprika. Blend to a fine consistency. Add in olive oil. Blend until the sauce has a smooth consistency.

2. Pat the chicken quarters dry and rub them down with salt and smoked paprika.

3. Pour Peri Peri Sauce on the chicken, and rub the marinade all over the chicken. With your fingers, loosen the skin from the chicken and make sure to get the marinade under the skin. Marinate for 4 to 24 hours, the longer the better.

4. When ready to roast, preheat the oven to 400°F (200°C).

5. Cover a sheet pan with aluminum foil for easy cleanup. Place an oven-safe wire rack on the sheet pan, and place the chicken quarters, well coated with Peri Peri Sauce, on the wire rack skin side up. Lightly brush olive oil all over them. (Do not discard the remaining Peri Peri Sauce marinade. You will use it later to baste the chicken as well as to make Peri Peri Dipping Sauce).

6. Bake for 30 minutes. Baste the chicken with reserved marinade. Bake for another 30 to 40 minutes, depending on the size of your chicken pieces, or until the chicken reads 180 to 185°F (82 to 85°C) on an instant read thermometer. Cook to 165°F (74°C) if cooking chicken breast.

7. Keep an eye on it towards the end of cooking time. If it's browning too quickly, cover it loosely with foil.

8. If necessary, you can also broil the chicken for more brown and crispy skin. Remove the chicken from the oven and let rest for 10 to 15 minutes before serving. Serve it with Peri Peri Dipping Sauce.

Dipping Sauce, optional

1. In a medium saucepan, heat olive oil in a saucepan. Add all remaining Peri Peri Sauce and simmer for 10 to 15 minutes. Add 1 tablespoon (15 milliliters) butter and cook for 5 minutes.

Grilling Method

1. Marinate the chicken as described above.

2. Have an adult preheat the grill to medium-high heat, around 350 to 375°F (180 to 190°C). The adult should place the chicken skin side down and grill with lid closed for 6 to 8 minutes. Flip the chicken over and continue cooking, flipping every 6 to 8 minutes, until internal temperature reaches 180 to 185°F (82 to 85°C).

3. When the chicken is done, remove to a platter and let rest for 10 to 15 minutes.

Goulash with Dumplings

 2 hours

 8 servings

Hungary

Ingredients

¼ cup (60 milliliters) all-purpose flour

1 Hungarian sweet paprika

1 ½ teaspoons (7.5 milliliters) salt

½ teaspoon (2.5 milliliters) Hungarian hot paprika

½ teaspoon (2.5 milliliters) black pepper

2 pounds (908 grams) beef stew meat

¼ cup (60 milliliters) vegetable oil, divided

1 large onion, chopped

4 garlic cloves, minced

28 ounces (794 grams) beef broth

14 ounces (397 grams) stewed tomatoes, undrained

1 cup (240 milliliters) water

1 tablespoon (15 milliliters) dried marjoram

1 green bell pepper, chopped

Sour cream

Dumplings

½ cup (120 milliliters) all-purpose flour

3 teaspoons (15 milliliters) baking powder

¼ teaspoon (1.2 milliliters) salt

2 tablespoons (30 milliliters) butter

1 egg

1 tablespoon (15 milliliters) milk

Directions

1. In a resealable food storage bag, combine flour, sweet paprika, salt, hot paprika, and black pepper. Add half of beef. Seal bag; shake to coat well. Remove beef to large bowl. Repeat with remaining beef.

2. In a Dutch oven over medium flame heat 1 ½ tablespoons (22.5 milliliters) oil. Add half of beef; cook until browned on all sides. Remove to large bowl. Repeat with 1 ½ tablespoons (22.5 milliliters) oil and remaining beef; remove to bowl.

3. Heat remaining 1 tablespoon (15 milliliters) oil in Dutch oven. Add onion and garlic; cook 8 minutes or until tender, stirring frequently.

4. Return beef with juices to Dutch oven. Add broth, tomatoes with juice, water, and marjoram; bring to a boil over medium-high heat. Reduce heat to low; cover and simmer 1 ½ hours until beef is tender, stirring once.

5. Stir in bell pepper; cover and cook about 8 minutes. Top with sour cream.

Dumplings

1. In a large mixing bowl, sift the flour. Mix in the baking powder and salt until well combined.

2. Rub the butter into the flour mixture. Stir in the egg and slowly add milk until a dough forms. Squeeze the dough together and roll it into 20 small balls. Twenty minutes prior to serving, add the dumplings to the goulash pot to cook.

Grilled Skirt Steak with Chimichurri Sauce

 25 minutes

 6 servings

Argentina

Ingredients

1 ½ pound (680 grams) skirt steak

1 tablespoon (15 milliliters) kosher salt

1 teaspoon (5 milliliters) black pepper, freshly ground

1 cup (240 milliliters) Chimichurri Sauce – recipe on page 73

Directions

1. Bring steak to room temperature and pat dry with a paper towel. Season both sides of the steak with salt and pepper.

2. An adult should start the outdoor grill or turn the stove grill pan to medium high heat. Cook the steak 3 to 4 minutes and turn over to cook the other side another 3 to 4 minutes depending on how well you like the meat cooked. Cook for less time for medium rare.

3. In addition to grilling the meat have an adult show you how to slice the steak properly and safely against the grain. Top with Chimichurri Sauce.

Chimichurri Sauce

 10 minutes

 6 servings

Argentina

Ingredients

1 cup (240 milliliters) fresh flat-leaf parsley. Trim thick stems and pack firmly.

4 garlic cloves

2 tablespoons (30 milliliters) fresh oregano

⅓ cup (80 milliliters) extra-virgin olive oil

2 tablespoons (30 milliliters) vinegar, or white or red wine

½ teaspoon (2.5 milliliters) sea salt

¼ teaspoon (1.2 milliliters) ground pepper

¼ teaspoon (1.2 milliliters) of red pepper flakes

Directions

1. Finely chop the parsley, garlic, and oregano together. (If you have a food processor, this is a good time to use it). Combine into a small bowl.
2. Mix in the olive oil, vinegar, salt, pepper, and red pepper flakes.
3. Serve fresh or chill in the fridge for up to 10 days. Make sure to serve at room temperature.

Birthday Noodles with Peanut Sauce

 30 minutes

 4 servings

China

Ingredients

2 tablespoons (30 milliliters) smooth peanut butter or sesame paste

¼ cup (60 milliliters) hot water

3 tablespoons (45 milliliters) soy sauce

1 teaspoon (5 milliliters) honey

4 cups (960 milliliters) cooked Chinese-style noodles or spaghetti

2 scallions, cut in ½ inch (1.25-centimeter) pieces

Bean sprouts, optional

Chopped peanuts, optional

Directions

1. In a large bowl, use a fork to stir the peanut butter or sesame paste with the water until it is creamy. Stir in the soy sauce and honey and set aside.

2. Drain the cooked noodles and add to the bowl with the peanut butter mixture and toss well.

3. Serve the noodles cold, topped with scallions, sprouts, or chopped peanuts.

Pasta with Tomato Sauce Allo Scarpariello

 25 minutes

 4 servings

Italy

Ingredients

11 ounces (312 grams) penne or spaghetti

9 ounces (255 grams) cherry tomatoes, cut in half

15 ounces (425 grams) tomato puree

¼ cup (60 milliliters) Parmigiano Reggiano cheese, grated

Basil, a handful, washed and torn into pieces

⅓ cup (80 milliliters) extra-virgin olive oil

Garlic, 1 clove, peeled

Fine salt, to taste

Directions

1. In a large pot, boil a pot of salted water.

2. In a large frying pan heat the olive oil and sauté garlic until it softens and add some basil.

3. Add the tomatoes. When the tomatoes have softened, pour in the tomato puree.

4. Simmer for approximately 15 minutes, remove the garlic, and add salt and pepper to taste.

5. Add pasta to the pot of boiling water and cook al dente. Drain it and add to the saucepan. Cook for 2 to 3 more minutes until the pasta is cooked.

6. Lower the heat, add the cheese, and combine with sauce and pasta. Cheese should melt completely.

7. Serve immediately with fresh basil and extra cheese.

Carrot, Apple, and Sweet Potato Tzimmes

Israel

 1 hour 20 minutes

 8 servings

Ingredients

3 large carrots, sliced

4 sweet potatoes, peeled and sliced

½ cup (120 milliliters) brown sugar, packed

¼ teaspoon (1.2 milliliters) salt

¼ teaspoon (1.2 milliliters) pepper

3 tablespoons (45 milliliters) margarine

3 Granny Smith apples, peeled and sliced

1 cup (240 milliliters) water

Directions

1. In a large saucepan over high heat, combine carrots, potatoes, and enough water to cover by 1 inch. Bring to a boil. Reduce heat to medium. Cover and cook 15 to 20 minutes, or until vegetables are tender, then drain.

2. In a 2 ½-quart (2.36-liter) baking dish, layer carrot slices to cover the bottom. Sprinkle ⅓ brown sugar, salt, and pepper on top and dot with 1 tablespoon (15 milliliters) margarine. Continue layering until all ingredients are used, sprinkling each layer with brown sugar, salt and pepper, and margarine. Pour 1 cup water over mixture.

3. Cover and bake 30 minutes at 350°F (180°C) until apples are tender. Uncover and bake 5 more minutes until top is golden.

Toad in the Hole

 55 minutes

 4 servings

Ingredients

1½ pounds (680 grams) pork sausages or sausage of your choice

2 teaspoons (10 milliliters) vegetable oil

Yorkshire Pudding Batter

1 cup (240 milliliters) eggs, lightly whisked

1 cup (240 milliliters) all-purpose flour

¼ cup (60 milliliters) water

¾ cup (175 milliliters) milk

1 tablespoon (15 milliliters) mayonnaise

½ teaspoon (2.5 milliliters) kosher salt

½ teaspoon (2.5 milliliters) black pepper

¼ cup (60 milliliters) vegetable oil

Onion Gravy

2 tablespoons (30 milliliters) unsalted butter

2 onions, halved and cut into ¼-inch (0.6-centimeter) wedges

1 garlic clove, minced

3 tablespoons (45 milliliters) all-purpose flour

2 cups (480 milliliters) beef stock

½ teaspoon (2.5 milliliters) Worcestershire sauce

½ teaspoon (2.5 milliliters) black pepper

¼ teaspoon (1.2 milliliters) kosher salt

Directions

For the Batter

1. In a medium bowl, whisk eggs, add in flour, and continue to whisk until lump free. Place in fridge.

2. Preheat oven to 425°F (220°C) and in a 9 x 13-inch (23 x 33-centimeter) pan. Heat the oil.

3. In a medium skillet, over medium heat add 2 teaspoons of water and sausages. Brown the sausage on all sides but do not cook through. Sausages will continue to cook in the oven. Remove sausages from skillet and transfer to plate. Leave the sausage drippings in the skillet as they will be used for the onion gravy.

4. Remove the batter from the fridge and whisk. Quickly assemble, carefully removing the hot pan from the oven. Place the sausages in the pan without touching the pan sides. Pour the batter in around the sausages (not on top).

5. Bake for 25 minutes on the top oven rack until the sides puff up and the color is golden brown. The top of the edges should be crispy. Serve immediately with Onion Gravy.

Onion Gravy

1. Reuse the medium skillet. Add onions and cook, stirring constantly, until browned (approximately 5 minutes). Add garlic and stir 30 seconds. Add flour and stir 1 minute until a lump-free gravy forms.

2. Slowly pour in the beef stock, stirring to combine. Add Worcestershire sauce, salt, and pepper. Bring to a simmer, stirring for 2 minutes until gravy thickens.

Desserts

Lamingtons

 50 minutes

 12 servings

Australia

Ingredients

Sponge Cake
½ cup (120 milliliters) all-purpose flour

½ cup (120 milliliters) cornstarch

½ teaspoon (2.5 milliliters) baking powder

3 large eggs

¼ cup (60 milliliters) superfine sugar

2 tablespoons (30 milliliters) milk

1 tablespoon (15 milliliters) butter

Chocolate Icing
½ cup (120 milliliters) cocoa powder

2 cups (480 milliliters) powdered sugar

2 tablespoons (30 milliliters) unsalted butter, melted

2 cups (480 milliliters) shredded coconut

TIP

To make superfine sugar put granulated sugar in a blender or food processor and blend on high speed until the sugar has a fine consistency but is not powdery. The ratio is 1:1 and for this recipe, ¼ cup of superfine sugar is needed and you should blend ¼ cup of granulated sugar.

Directions

1. Preheat oven to 350°F (180°C). Grease an 8-inch (20-centimeter) square cake pan and set aside.
2. In a large mixing bowl, sift flour, cornstarch, and baking powder and set aside.
3. In a separate mixing bowl, add eggs and whisk until the eggs start to thicken and foam forms. Add sugar, one tablespoon at a time.
4. Continue to beat until the eggs thicken, approximately 5 to 8 minutes. You'll know the eggs are ready when you can draw the number 8 on top and it stays for 1 to 2 seconds.
5. In a small microwave-safe bowl, heat milk and butter for 30 seconds until butter is melted. Set aside to cool.
6. Gently add the sifted flour mixture into the eggs. Add the butter mixture and fold in until gently combined. Do not overmix.
7. Add mixture to prepared cake pan. Bake for 20 to 23 minutes or until cake gently springs back when lightly touched on top. Leave to cool completely.
8. To make the chocolate icing, sift cocoa powder and icing sugar. Add melted butter and milk and stir until chocolate is smooth.
9. Cut sponge cake into 12 squares. Carefully and quickly dip each piece of cake into chocolate, let the extra chocolate drip off, and then sprinkle tops with coconut. Transfer to a cake rack to dry.
10. Repeat with remaining cake squares.

Pretzels

 50 minutes   2 large pretzels

Germany

Ingredients

2 ½ tablespoons (37.5 milliliters) molasses

1 ½ cups (360 milliliters) warm water

2 ¼ teaspoons (11.2 milliliters) active dry yeast

3 tablespoons (45 milliliters) butter, softened, more for serving

4 cups (960 milliliters) all-purpose flour, plus more for dusting

¼ teaspoon (1.2 milliliters) kosher salt

Pretzel salt for sprinkling, optional

Pretzel Wash

2 tablespoons (30 milliliters) baking soda

1 cup (240 milliliters) water

TIP

For more servings: divide dough into 8 to 10 equal portions, invite some friends over, and have a pretzel making party. Oven temperature and cooking time will be the same as for 2 large pretzels.

Directions

1. Preheat oven to 450°F (230°C). Heat a baking stone or a sheet pan.

2. In a large bowl stir together molasses, yeast, and water. Let sit until foam forms, approximately 10 minutes.

3. Add in butter, flour, and salt, stirring until a dough forms. You can use clean hands to mix until combined and then transfer dough to a lightly floured flat surface. Knead by hand until dough is smooth and elastic, about 8 minutes.

4. Carefully cut the dough in half, working with one piece at a time. Roll the dough out into a 4-inch (10-centimeter) rope about 1-inch (2.5-centimeters) thick.

5. Transfer the rope to a sheet of parchment paper. Keeping the center of the rope on the paper, pick up both ends of the rope, cross one end over the other about 2 inches (5 centimeters) from the ends, and twist. Attach each end to the sides of the pretzel. Look at the photo of the finished pretzel to see how to shape.

6. Repeat with remaining dough and cover both pretzels with a damp towel and set aside to rest and rise in a warm place for 20 minutes.

7. In a 2-quart (1.8-liter) saucepan over medium-high heat, bring baking soda and water to a boil. Simmer, stirring until baking soda is dissolved.

8. Brush each pretzel generously with the baking soda wash, sprinkle with pretzel salt, if using, and carefully make a 6-inch (15-centimeter) slash ¼-inch (0.6-centimeters) deep across the bottom of the pretzel.

9. One at a time, slide each pretzel onto parchment paper and move onto the baking stone or sheet pan. Place into preheated oven and bake for 15 minutes or until dark brown. Let cool for about 10 minutes. Traditional German pretzels are served warm with butter.

Boston Cream Pie

 2 hours

 10 servings

USA

Ingredients

2 large eggs, room temperature

1 cup (240 milliliters) cane sugar

½ cup (120 milliliters) whole milk

5 tablespoons (75 milliliters) unsalted butter

1 cup (240 milliliters) all-purpose flour plus 2 tablespoons (30 milliliters)

1¼ teaspoons (6.2 milliliters) baking powder

¼ teaspoon (1.2 milliliters) kosher salt

2 teaspoons (10 milliliters) vanilla extract

¼ cup (60 milliliters) heavy whipping cream

4 ounces (110 grams) bittersweet chocolate, chopped

Pastry Cream

6 egg yolks, room temperature

⅔ cup (160 milliliters) sugar

¼ cup (60 milliliters) corn starch

1 tablespoon (15 milliliters) vanilla extract

2 cups (480 milliliters) whole milk

1 tablespoon (15 milliliters) butter

Directions

For the Pastry Cream

1. Pour the milk into a medium saucepan, heat, then place over medium heat and bring to a boil. Immediately turn off the heat and set.

2. In a large bowl, whisk the egg yolks and sugar until light and thickened. Sift in the cornstarch and whisk vigorously until no lumps remain. Whisk in ¼ cup (60 milliliters) of the hot milk mixture until incorporated. Whisk in the remaining hot milk mixture, reserving the pot for later.

3. Pour the mixture through a strainer back into the pot. Cook over medium-high heat, whisking constantly, until thickened and slowly boiling. Cook while whisking for 1 to 2 more minutes after thickened and boiling. Remove from the heat and stir in the butter. Let cool slightly then cover with plastic wrap, lightly pressing the plastic against the surface to prevent a skin from forming. Chill in the fridge.

For the Cake

1. Preheat oven to 350°F (180°C). Spray a 8-inch (20-centimeters) round cake pan with baking spray or butter and flour it. Line bottom with parchment paper and spray again.

2. Combine flour, baking powder, and salt in a bowl, then whisk together and set aside.

3. In a stand mixer fitted with a whisk attachment or large mixing bowl if using a hand mixer, add eggs and sugar. Beat on medium speed until pale, thick, and fluffy, about 4 minutes. Beater should leave a trail in eggs when lifted.

4. Meanwhile, in a glass measuring cup, combine milk and butter. Microwave on high in 30 second intervals until butter is melted and milk is steaming.

5. With mixer on low speed, gradually add flour mixture to egg mixture, beating just until combined. Stir vanilla into hot milk mixture. Slowly pour hot milk mixture into egg mixture, beating until fully combined. Batter will look like thick pancake batter and have bubbles on top. Scrape the sides of the bowl and fold batter a few times to ensure it's fulling combined. Pour batter into the prepared cake pan.

6. Bake until a toothpick inserted in center comes out clean and cake begins pulling away from sides of pan, about 33 minutes. Let cool in pan for a few minutes then invert onto a wire rack to cool completely.

For the Assembly

1. Cut cake in half horizontally. Place bottom half, cut side up on a serving plate. Spread the chilled, thickened pastry cream over cake, leaving a 1-inch (2.5-centimeter) border. Top with remaining cake half and gently press down to spread filling to edge. Place in fridge and chill for at least 2 hours or overnight; cover with plastic or a cloche if chilling for more than 2 hours.

For the Ganache

1. When ready to serve, place cream in a microwave-safe bowl; microwave cream and optional corn syrup until steaming, about 1 minute. Add chopped chocolate and let stand for 5 minutes. Stir chocolate and cream mixture until smooth. Pour over top of cake, spreading to edges.

No Bake Strawberry Mochi

 40 minutes   4 servings

Japan

Ingredients

1 cup (240 milliliters) of Mochiko rice flour or Tapioca flour

2 cups (480 milliliters) of sugar

¾ cup (175 milliliters) of water

Cornstarch (to dust the dough)

½ cup (110 grams) strawberries, chopped

Directions

1. Mix the Mochiko rice flour and water together, until it reaches a dough-like consistency. Add more water if needed.
2. Steam the dough for 20 minutes.
3. Transfer the mochi into a pot and add ⅓ of the sugar in low-medium heat. Mix until it's completely dissolved. Do this again until you finish all the sugar. This will keep the mochi chewy.
4. Once it is sticky and shiny, transfer it to the tray covered with parchment paper and cornstarch.
5. Once the dough has cooled, dust your hands with some cornstarch and start shaping the dough. They should be a little smaller than a golf ball.
6. You can add all sorts fillings inside your mochis, from ice cream to fruit. For this recipe, strawberry is used.
7. Once you wrap the dough over your filling, you can eat the treat right away. Freeze for future if you choose.

Churros

 35 minutes

 12 servings

Spain

Ingredients

½ cup (120 milliliters) water

½ cup (120 milliliters) 2% milk

1 tablespoon canola oil

¼ teaspoon (1.2 milliliters) salt

1½ cups (360 milliliters) all-purpose flour

1 large egg, room temperature

¼ teaspoon (1.2 milliliters) grated lemon zest

2 cups additional oil for frying

½ cup (120 milliliters) sugar

¼ teaspoon (1.2 milliliters) ground cinnamon

Directions

1. In a large saucepan, bring the water, milk, oil, and salt to a boil. Add flour all at once and stir until a smooth ball forms. Transfer to a large bowl; let stand for 5 minutes.

2. Beat on medium-high speed for 1 minute or until the dough softens. Add egg and lemon zest; beat for 1 to 2 minutes. Set aside to cool.

3. In a deep cast-iron or heavy skillet, heat 1 inch oil to 375°F (190°C). Insert a large star tip in a pastry bag; fill with dough. On a baking sheet, pipe dough into 4-inch (10-centimeter) strips.

4. Transfer strips to skillet and fry until golden brown on both sides. Drain on paper towels. Combine the sugar and cinnamon; sprinkle over churros. Serve warm.

Champurrado (Mexican Hot Chocolate)

 10 minutes   4 servings

Mexico

Ingredients

¼ cup (60 milliliters) baking cocoa

2 tablespoons (30 milliliters) brown sugar

1 cup (240 milliliters) boiling water

¼ teaspoon (1.2 milliliters) ground cinnamon

Dash ground cloves or nutmeg

3 cups (720 milliliters) whole milk

1 teaspoon (5 milliliters) vanilla extract

Whipped cream

Whole cinnamon sticks

Directions

1. In a small saucepan, mix cocoa and sugar; stir in water. Bring to a boil. Reduce heat; cook 2 minutes, stirring constantly.

2. Add cinnamon and cloves; stir in milk. Simmer 5 minutes (do not boil). Whisk in vanilla. Pour hot chocolate into mugs; top with whipped cream. Use cinnamon sticks for stirrers. Sprinkle top layer with chocolate flakes or dust with cocoa powder just prior to serving.

Yema Balls

 1 hour

 30 balls (depending on size)

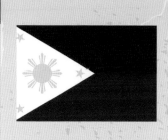

Philippines

Ingredients

2 tablespoons (30 milliliters) unsalted butter, melted

10 ounce (283 grams) can condensed milk

3 egg yolks, from large eggs

¼ teaspoon (1.2 milliliters) salt

Sugar for coating

Oil for greasing

TIP
Crush your favorite nuts and roll the balls around in the nuts for a crunchy topping.

Directions

1. In a small pot, add butter and milk and stir until combined.

2. Add egg yolks and salt and stir until mixture thickens, about 20 minutes.

3. Lightly grease a platter and pour mixture onto it and allow to cool completely.

4. Once mixture is cool and firm to the touch, scoop 1 teaspoon (5 milliliters) of the mixture, with clean hands, roll into a small ball. Coat in sugar and serve.

Sopaipillas

 45 minutes

 6-8 servings

Chile

Ingredients

9 ounces (255 grams) zapallo squash, peeled, seeded, and cut into chunks

4 ¼ cups (1020 milliliters) all-purpose flour

1 teaspoon (5 milliliters) baking soda

1 teaspoon (5 milliliters) salt

10 tablespoons (150 milliliters) butter, melted

2 cups (480 milliliters) canola oil for pan-frying

TIP
Zapallo, or Jamaican pumpkin, is a type of winter squash from South America. If it's not available, small sugar pumpkins make a good substitute.

Directions

1. In a medium saucepan over high heat, place squash, cover with water, and bring to a boil over medium-high heat. Cook until zapallo is soft and easily pierced with a fork, 15 to 20 minutes. Drain and allow to cool slightly.

2. Mix flour, baking soda, and salt together in a mixing bowl, and set aside. Stir together squash and melted butter. Stir the flour mixture into the butter mixture until blended. Turn the dough out onto a lightly floured surface and knead until soft and smooth, adding a little more flour if necessary. Cover dough with a towel and allow to rest 15 minutes.

3. Roll out the dough to 1/8-inch (0.3-centimeter) thick, and cut into 3-inch (7.5-centimeter) diameter circles. Poke each circle a few times with a fork to make holes and prevent rising.

4. Pour oil into a large, deep skillet and heat over medium-high heat until hot, 385°F (196°C). Place several of the dough circles into hot oil; cook until lightly browned, 3 to 4 minutes. Drain on paper towels. Cook remainder of dough circles in batches.

ANZAC Biscuits (Golden Oatmeal Cookies)

Australia

 30 minutes

 16 to 18 cookies

Ingredients

1 cup (240 milliliters) all-purpose flour

1 cup (240 milliliters) rolled oats

1 cup (240 milliliters) dried coconut, unsweetened

3/4 cup (180 milliliters) white sugar, fine

5 ounces (140 grams) unsalted butter

4 tablespoons (60 milliliters) golden syrup

1 teaspoon (5 milliliters) baking soda

TIP
Golden syrup - best substitute 1 tablespoon (15 milliliters) light molasses + 3 tablespoons (45 milliliters) honey or light corn syrup.

Directions

1. Preheat oven to 350°F (180°C).

2. Line 2 baking trays with silicone or parchment paper.

3. In a medium bowl add flour, oats, coconut, and sugar and combine.

4. Place butter and golden syrup in a saucepan over medium-high heat and stir until butter has melted.

5. Add baking soda and stir to combine. It will fizz up; this is normal. Immediately remove from heat.

6. Pour butter mixture into flour and mix until just combined.

7. Roll 1 tablespoon (15 milliliters) mixture into balls, flatten into patties. Place balls, 1-inch (2.5-centimeters) apart, on prepared trays.

8. Bake for 15 minutes, swapping trays halfway during cooking, or until deep golden. Cook for 3 fewer minutes if you prefer chewier cookies.

9. Transfer to a wire rack to cool. They harden as they cool!

Celebrations Around the World

Bastille Day – France – Every year on July 14th, France celebrates Bastille Day. This marks the anniversary of the Storming of the Bastille on July 14, 1789, which was a turning point for the success of the French Revolution and the end of absolute rule by monarchs. Paris has the country's largest celebration with a morning military ceremony followed by a huge military parade down the Avenue des Champs Élysées and a flyover by military aircraft. The celebration concludes with the spectacular Bastille Day fireworks show at the Eiffel Tower on the Champ de Mars, which starts at 11 p.m. It lights up the sky for half an hour. Families celebrate with a simple picnic in parks around the city. Crepes, croissants, brioche, wine, bread and cheese, and quiche are favorites.

Carnival – Italy – Carnival is celebrated 40 days before Easter and lasts two or three weeks. It is a farewell party to eat, drink, and have fun before the limitations and solemnity of Lent. Throughout Italy, celebrations include parades, wearing elaborate costumes, dancing in the streets, and lots of colorful confetti. Historically, masks were a crucial part of Carnival, as anonymity allowed partygoers to be whomever they wanted to be. Today, wearing elaborate masks allows people to display their artistic expression and look good. The city of Venice has the largest celebration with opulent, invitation-only masquerade balls, candlelit boat parades, street performances, and concerts. Eating lots of sweets is something everyone enjoys as sweets consumption is not permitted during Lent. There is an overabundance of classic Italian treats including frappé, tiramisu, pannacotta, and Castagnole (a fried sweet dough), and Italian wine.

Chinese New Year – China – Typically, Chinese New Year begins between late January and late February, depending on the cycles of the moon. The celebration's focus is on removing the bad and the old and welcoming the new and the good. It's a time to worship ancestors, exorcise evil spirits, and pray for good harvests. Celebrations include firecrackers, dragon dances, fireworks, and red clothes and decorations. Red envelopes (*hongbao* in Mandarin and *lai see* in Cantonese) are small, red and gold packets that contain money, and are given to children, family members, friends, and employees as a symbol of good luck. In Chinese culture, red is associated with energy, happiness, and good luck. A big family feast includes noodles (to symbolize living long and prospering), dumplings (to symbolize wealth and prosperity), and fresh fruit (to represent life and new beginnings), and tea (for hospitality).

Day of the Dead – Mexico – Dia de los Muertos is celebrated on November 1st and 2nd. It is believed the spirits of the dead return home and spend time with their relatives on these two days. It is common to see *calaveras* (skulls) as decorations. These can be made of papier-mâché, clay, wood, metal, or cut-out tissue paper. Often, they are made of sugar and decorated with colored icing, flowers, or metallic colored foils. It is a joyful time that helps people remember the deceased and celebrate their memory. To welcome the spirits, the family builds altars in their honor. These altars have different components, which vary from one culture to another. Mostly, they include candles, photos of the deceased, *papel picado* (cut tissue-paper designs), as well as food and beverage offerings for the dead. Food is key to the celebration, with *ofrendas* (offerings) of Pan de Muertos (Bread of the Dead), Pozole, and *champurrado* (Mexican hot chocolate).

Diwali – India – The Hindu festival of lights takes place every autumn between October and November. It is one of the major religious festivals in Hinduism, Jainism, and Sikhism. The name is derived from the Sanskrit term *dipavali,* meaning "row of lights." It symbolizes the spiritual victory of light over dark, good over evil, and knowledge over ignorance. People take part in festive gatherings, fireworks displays, feasts, and prayer during this five day festival. Celebratory foods include curried chickpeas, *kheer* (rice pudding), *Nan Khatai* (cardamom biscuits), and herby paneer parcels and delicious lassis.

Oktoberfest – Germany – Oktoberfest is held annually from the Saturday after September 15th to the first Sunday in October. It attracts more than 6 million visitors to Germany from all around the world. Oktoberfest was first celebrated in Munich in 1810, to honor Prince Ludwig's marriage to Princess Therese von Sachsen-Hildburghausen. It was a weeklong celebration that concluded with an exciting horse race. Today, the main festival celebrating Bavarian life and history takes place in Munich with smaller celebrations throughout Germany. It is the biggest beer festival in the world and is known for its traditional Bavarian costumes and delicious German food. Many women wear *dirndl* dresses and men wear *lederhosen* (traditional leather britches). *Kartoffelpuffer* (potato pancakes), Bratwurst, *Käsespätzle* (cheese spaetzle) and large *Bretzein* (pretzels) are enjoyed, often with a beer.

St. Patrick's Day – Ireland – Since the ninth or tenth century, people in Ireland have observed the Roman Catholic feast day of St. Patrick on March 17. What was once a religious event has now become a day of cultural celebration. The first St. Patrick's Day parade took place not in Ireland but in America. It was held on March 17, 1601 in a Spanish colony that is now known as St. Augustine, Florida. This celebration was organized by the colony's Irish vicar Ricardo Artur. More than a century later, homesick Irish soldiers serving in the English military marched in New York City (NYC) on March 17, 1772, to honor the Irish patron saint. The holiday has evolved into a celebration of Irish culture with parades, music, dancing, and drinking. And lots of green shamrocks and leprechauns everywhere. Today, more than 200 countries celebrate, and the NYC parade is the largest St. Patrick's Day parade in the world. Irish Soda Bread, Corned Beef, Cabbage, and Potatoes, and Irish coffee are enjoyed in abundance.

The Culinary Passport Series

978-1-943016-24-2
978-1-943016-27-3
978-1-943016-25-9

978-1-943016-26-6
978-1-943016-29-7
978-1-943016-30-3
978-1-943016-23-5

Discover recipes from all over the world!

KITCHEN INK

Travel around the world from your kitchen.

Chef José Andrés

Chef José Andrés, born and trained in Spain, moved to the US at age 21. He soon settled in Washington, DC, and began volunteering at DC Central Kitchen, where he started to think big about philanthropy. Over the course of his career as a chef and restaurateur, he saw the role of cooks – and the power of food – to change the world. This path inspired José to found World Central Kitchen (WCK) in 2010 after a devastating earthquake in Haiti, with the support of his wife Patricia, as well as his business partner Rob Wilder and his wife Robin. Since then, he's pursued a mission to fulfill the words of John Steinbeck: **"Wherever there's a fight so that hungry people may eat … we'll be there."**

Where do you want to
travel next?